"they look at you and are revulsed.

"They call you *freaks* and they think your handicaps are all there is to who you *are*!

"We can prove them *wrong*. We can turn their scorn to grudging admiration.

"*Join* with me, my friends. *Together* we can make a *difference*."

— from "The Secret Origin of the Doom Patrol."

doom

PATROL

crawling from the **wreckage**

writer   grant morrison

pencillers   richard case

doug braithwaite

inkers   scott hanna

carlos garzon

john nyberg

colorists   daniel vozzo

michele wolfman

letterer   john workman

original series covers

richard case

scott hanna

carlos garzon

nobody

Karen Berger VP-Executive Editor Robert Greenberger, Mark Waid Editors-original series Bob Kahan Editor-collected edition Robbin Brosterman Senior Art Director Paul Levitz President & Publisher Georg Brewer VP-Design & Retail Product Development Richard Bruning Senior VP-Creative Director Patrick Caldon Senior VP-Finance & Operations Chris Caramalis VP-Finance Terri Cunningham VP-Managing Editor Alison Gill VP-Manufacturing Rich Johnson VP-Book Trade Sales Hank Kanalz VP-General Manager, WildStorm Lillian Laserson Senior VP & General Counsel Jim Lee Editorial Director-WildStorm David McKillips VP-Advertising & Custom Publishing John Nee VP-Business Development Gregory Noveck Senior VP-Creative Affairs Cheryl Rubin Senior VP-Brand Management Bob Wayne VP-Sales & Marketing

DOOM PATROL: CRAWLING FROM THE WRECKAGE

wants to be a human brain in a robot body

or

why this isn't a super-hero comic, and why that's good

But enough about DOOM PATROL; let's talk about me.

When I was a kid, like millions of others, I would pin a red bath towel to my collar and imitate Georg Reeves's springboard Superman takeoffs. Other days, unlike millions of others, I might clench my right fist and spin my arm like a windmill, creating a miniature tornado that could uproot trees, in imitation of the Flash's super-speed. Sometimes, like no other kid before or since, I would wear my sport coat and clip-on necktie and dart for cover from bush to car to tree as I believed James Bond would if he ever ended up in my neighborhood. Besides absorbing and reliving the adventures of these beloved heroes, I also read Arnold Drake and Bruno Premiani's DOOM PATROL each month — but I never wrapped my head in bandages and feigned weakness in 60-second bursts as a radioactive parasite fled my body to perform routine rescues that I could only watch. I never wished that isolated parts of my body could grow or shrink if only I could concentrate hard enough. I certainly never wanted to burn to a crisp in an auto wreck so my brain could be transplanted into a clunky robot body with a steamshovel jaw.

And that's why the Doom Patrol — Larry Trainor, Negative Man; Rita Farr, Elasti-Girl; and Cliff Steele, Robotman — weren't really super-heroes, despite their names and the way they looked. Part of the function of a super-hero is to give us a refuge from our normalcy, an identification with something wonderful, a secret airborne headquarters from which we can look down at our friends, families and authority figures — especially authority figures — and feel pity for their tragic lack of special gifts.

Disguised as a regular comic book, DOOM PATROL subverted this drive. Compared to the omniplegic Cliff and the infected Larry, normal people were to be envied, not pitied. In a similar way, a nine-year-old who windmills his arm in the direction of an old elm tree on a busy city street corner in broad daylight might secretly envy normal people as they puzzle at him from their Valiants and Corvairs. Maybe you have felt this envy, too.

So if the Doom Patrol aren't super-heroes, I guess they're people, just like you and me, or at least like me. They don't look like anything that can exist, but maybe the feelings that come with the full-body bandages and the steamshovel jaw and the ankles like sequoia trunks are as genuine as the last time you compared yourself to a stranger and came up short. Maybe the untroubled normalcy we project onto others is what's so preposterous. Maybe the Doom Patrol make perfect sense.

Mind you, I'm not claiming to have developed this analysis 29 years ago while amputating the pet parakeet's wings for my homemade Hawkman helmet ˚; all I really knew then was that the DP were gross and made me feel weird, and that I went out of my way to buy every issue.

It's almost thirty years later, and Grant Morrison and Richard Case have given us a new Doom Patrol (whose story begins in this volume), and interested readers have an opportunity to feel gross and weird all over again. Like the original version, Grant and Richard's Doom Patrol sort of resemble other action heroes on the surface, but fall pathetically out of step once the chase music starts. Crime-fighters who fly, shrink and stretch once again seem ordinary by comparison, and ordinary people lucky. Their first full storyline, "Crawling From the Wreckage," begins in one hospital and cuts abruptly to another, racking up infirmities in the first few pages like most comic books go through super-powers.

In the place of Rita, who could pass for regular folks, and whose power was never all that horrible, there's Kay Challis, the unforgettable Crazy Jane, whose paranormal "gifts" are limited only by the number of personalities serving time inside her head. As her story opens, there are 64 in attendance.

Larry Trainor and the super-parasite are still together, joined by the unwilling Dr. Eleanor Poole to form Rebis, the radioactive hermaphrodite who just doesn't sound like Larry anymore. That bothers our old friend Cliff; he's still the same, but when you start out as a leaky gray sponge in a prosthetic body there's not much room to deteriorate.

Also along for the plunge are Niles Caulder, the difficult genius who founded the Doom Patrol; Rhea Jones, a comatose girl who seems to be sleeping her way toward a frightening destiny; and the lovable Dorothy Spinner, an ape-faced adolescent whose inner life can manifest itself for all to see — a "gift" that would have most teenagers clawing the asylum gate for entry.

The only member with what I would call healthy, average super-powers — Joshua Clay, a physician who can fly and shoot some kind of ray-blasts from his fists — is too freaked-out by all of this to let himself use them. He'd rather stand by for the inevitable medical emergencies and perform routine tasks for the Chief in the meantime.

As tedious as that sounds, we can't blame Josh for trading his tights for an apron when we consider the opposition. The Doom Patrol has never been lucky enough to face mere jewel thieves who dress like playing cards, or masked kidnappers who messenger easy clues to their whereabouts to the commissioner's office. Their rogues gallery is more likely to include the imaginary world that threatens to become real, supplanting our own reality; the unattended machine that could make dreams come true; the bloodthirsty omnipotent who claims to be God, and who's to say for sure he's lying?

For all of these dangerous encounters, for all of our heroes' disorders and infirmities, for all of their fear and heartbreak, one of the best features of Grant's DOOM PATROL scripts is what's missing from them. Another writer working with the same ingredients might have inflated the stories with the familiar grim-and-gritty solemnity of the DARK KNIGHT/WATCHMEN imitators. Don't bother looking for the (yawn) clipped, first-person angst, the (groan) balletic violence, the (sob) dead

sidekicks, the (ah-chooo!) anguished resignation that worked so well in those projects and has seldom done the job since. Grant is too playful and hard-working a writer for any of this; in its place, you'll find pleasure in the strange workings of his universe, a fondness for its inhabitants, and a straightforward presentation rare in comics today.

A large share of the credit for that presentation must go to Richard Case's style and storytelling. Watching him grow from the raw but confident talent seen here to the inspired practitioner of the current run has been one of DOOM PATROL's most satisfying rewards.

The result of Richard and Grant's hard work is one of my favorite comics ever. A couple of years after these stories were first published, I had the good fortune to become editor of the regular monthly title. No matter what happens, I intend to hang on to DOOM PATROL until they pry it from my cold, dead fingers.

But enough about me; let's read DOOM PATROL.

—Tom Peyer

1992

"All the time I've been away,
I've been studying reports,
filing information, making

preparations"

roaringraringracing haring home on the homestretch now and the wind in my ears the sound of the crowd

200 on the speedo...210... 215...220...and oh the sky runningspilling blue smoke

every-thing moves

so

slow

and i should have seen it

the oil slick

i should have

saved it

i saved it

i saved the beautiful bit

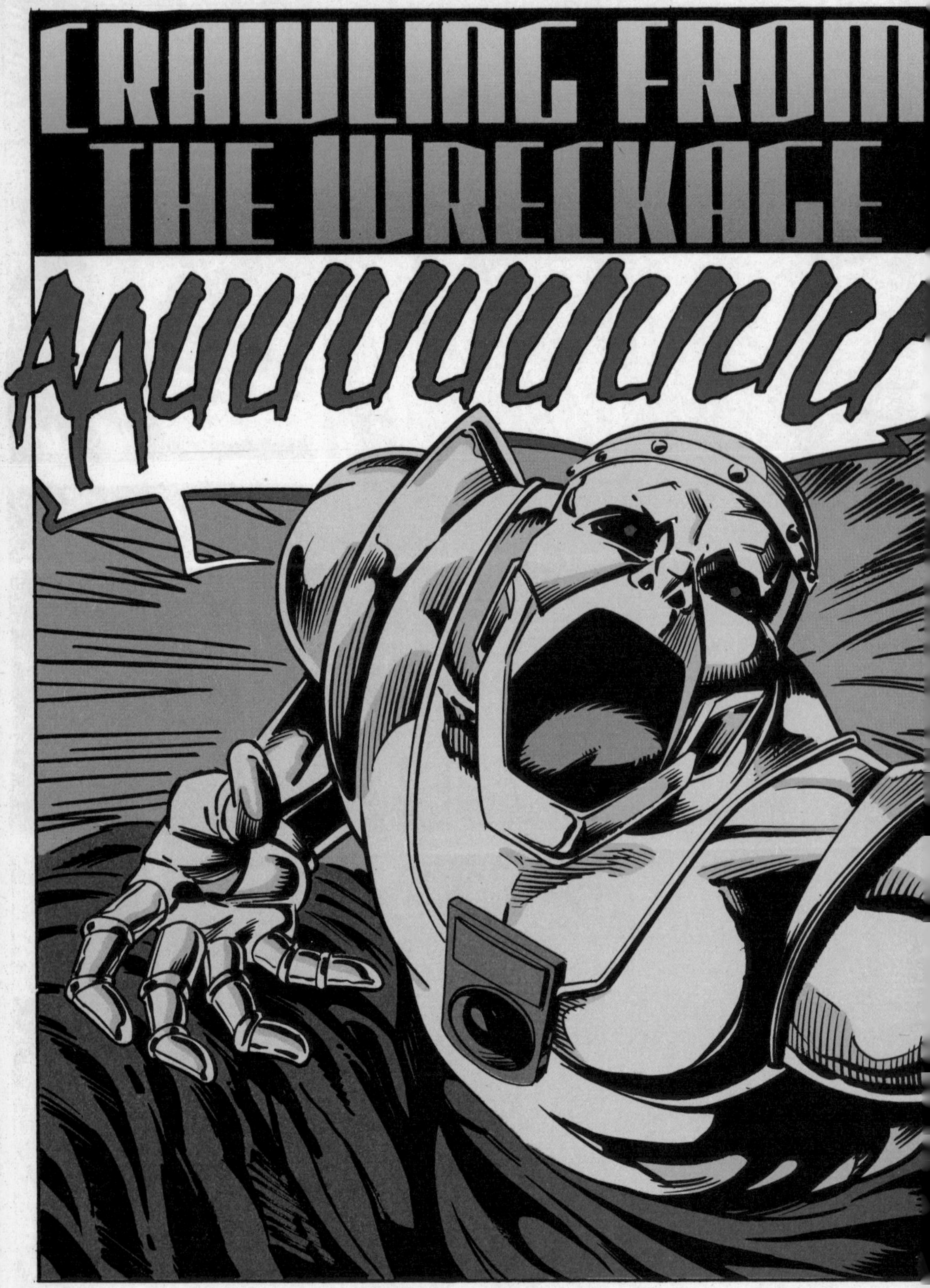
CRAWLING FROM THE WRECKAGE
AAUUUUUUUUUUU

WELL, NOW...

DREAMING ABOUT OUR *ACCIDENT* AGAIN, ARE WE?

THAT'S WHAT HAPPENS...

...WHEN WE REFUSE TO TAKE OUR *MEDICATION.*

GET LOST.

COME ON NOW, RISE AND SHINE! I'VE BROUGHT YOU A FRESH *NUTRIENT TANK.*

NOW WHERE ARE WE GOING TO PUT IT?

"WE" CAN SHOVE IT WHERE THE SUN DOESN'T SHINE.

HARD.

YOU'VE GOT A REAL BAD ATTITUDE PROBLEM, MISTER. I'LL TELL YOU THAT FOR *NOTHING.*

SHUT UP.

GET OUT.

JUST LEAVE ME ALONE.

13

ALAMANCE
MEMORIAL
HOSPITAL

TRANSPLANT
9C

...YES, THIS IS *ELEANOR POOLE*...WELL, IF YOU LIKE...*THE* ELEANOR POOLE.

...OF COURSE... WELL, *YOUR* REPUTATION PRECEDES YOU ...I'M AFRAID SO, YEAH...

WHAT?... YOU READ *THAT*? OH, WELL...NOW YOU'RE EMBARRASSING *ME*.

ANYWAY, WHAT CAN I DO FOR YOU?

LARRY TRAINOR, RIGHT.

YEAH...UH, LISTEN. SOMETHING'S JUST... YEAH.

GREAT TALKING TO YOU, TOO... SURE, FINE.

YOU, TOO.

BYE.

WELL, YOU'LL BE GLAD TO KNOW THAT HE'S IN GREAT SHAPE AND WE HOPE TO SEND HIM HOME IN THE NEXT DAY OR TWO...THAT'S RIGHT...

CAUTION WET FLOOR

14

SO YOU WON'T JOIN IN MY NEW DOOM PATROL, IS THAT WHAT YOU'RE SAYING?

LOOK, THE DOOM PATROL'S *DEAD,* CAULDER. WHY NOT LET IT REST IN PEACE THIS TIME?

AND AS FOR ME, I'M *FINISHED* WITH ALL THIS, REALLY.

IT'S JUST NOT *FUNNY* ANYMORE.

ARANI'S DEAD, SCOTT'S DEAD, RHEA'S IN A COMA, LARRY'S HOSPITALIZED, VAL'S RESIGNED, AND NO ONE'S EVEN *MENTIONED* CLIFF...

CLIFF SIGNED HIMSELF INTO A PSYCHIATRIC HOSPITAL. HE FELT HE NEEDED *HELP.*

I SHOULDN'T WORRY. I'VE ASKED A GOOD FRIEND TO PAY HIM A VISIT.

AND I'M SURE IT WON'T BE LONG BEFORE *ROBOTMAN* IS BACK WITH US AGAIN.

JEEZ, BUT YOU'RE AN *ICEMAN,* CAULDER.

WHY THANK YOU, JOSHUA. AND PLEASE...

...CALL ME *CHIEF.*

16

...IK. ...IK.CHICKEN THAT LAYS AN EGG WITH THE FACE OF *CHRIST* IMPRINTED ON THE SHELL, INHUMAN VOICES WHISPERING THROUGH THE STATIC ON AN EMPTY RADIO WAVEBAND.

DON'T THESE THINGS *FASCINATE* YOU, JOSHUA?

NOT REALLY. I CAN GET *THAT* KIND OF STUFF FROM THE *NATIONAL ENQUIRER.*

AND I DON'T SEE WHAT IT HAS TO DO WITH THE *DOOM PATROL.*

I HAVE PLANS, JOSHUA. ALL THE TIME I'VE BEEN AWAY, I'VE BEEN STUDYING REPORTS, FILING INFORMA-TION, MAKING *PREPARA-TIONS.*

AND DON'T TELL ME—WHETHER I LIKE IT OR NOT, I'M PART OF THE BIG PLAN, RIGHT?

OH, YES.

YOU *ALL* ARE.

MR. STEELE?

MR. STEELE, YOU HAVE A VISITOR HERE TO SEE YOU.

CLIFF?

CLIFF. IT'S ME.

IT'S WILL. WILL MAGNUS.

YOU REMEMBER ME, DON'T YOU?

I MADE THE METAL MEN, CLIFF.

I MADE YOUR BODY, TOO, REMEMBER?

CLIFF?

UH... RIGHT.

YEAH.

18

I KNEW I RECOGNIZED THAT PATRONIZING TONE FROM SOME- WHERE.

THERE'S NO NEED FOR THAT, CLIFF.

WHEN I HEARD YOU'D COME IN HERE, I...WELL, I UNDERSTAND WHAT YOU'RE GOING THROUGH. I'VE BEEN THERE.

AND I THINK YOU AND I CAN LICK THIS THING TOGETHER.

HOW ABOUT IT, CLIFF?

YOU'RE A GOOD GUY, DOC.

YOU'RE SENSITIVE AND CARING AND COMPASSIONATE,

AND IF I COULD, I'D SPEW IN YOUR FACE.

19

ALAMANCE
MEMORIAL
HOSPITAL

TOMORROW? AND I WAS JUST GETTING USED TO ALL THE *ATTENTION*.

WE NOTICED.

SO GIVE IT TO ME STRAIGHT, DOC.

SAME AS EVERYONE ELSE, LARRY. NO MORE, NO LESS.

YOU STILL HAVE WHAT EVERYONE'S CALLING THE "HERO GENE," BUT APART FROM THAT, YOU'RE PERFECTLY NORMAL.

YOU BET I AM!

WHEN ALL THIS IS OVER, YOU AND ME OUGHT TO GET TOGETHER, DOCTOR, YOU KNOW THAT?

LISTEN, IT COULD BE OVER SOONER THAN YOU THINK...

...IF MY BOYFRIEND HEARS YOU TALKING LIKE THAT.

HOW LONG HAVE I GOT?

AND REMEMBER, THAT BELL BESIDE THE BED'S ONLY FOR *EMERGENCIES*, OKAY?

YEAH. SURE THING, DOCTOR.

SEE YOU.

LAARREEE

20

LAARRREEEE

OH, GOD.

WHAT DO YOU WANT?

...WHAT...

OH, GOD.

IAMTHE SPIRITINTHE BOTTLETHE INVISIBLEFIRE THATWORKSIN SECRETTHERE ISTICKAMONG THEROOTSOF THEOAKTREE

OPENTHE WINDOWNOW

OPENTHE WINDOWLAR RYLETMEIN

LETMEIN

LET

ME

IN

...WHY D'YOU KEEP FOLLOWING ME ABOUT, MAGNUS?

WHY DON'T YOU JUST LEAVE ME ALONE?

YOU'VE GOT TO PULL YOURSELF THROUGH THIS, CLIFF!

BELIEVE ME, I KNOW WHAT IT'S LIKE...

HOW THE HELL CAN YOU "KNOW WHAT IT'S LIKE"!?

HOW CAN YOU KNOW WHAT IT'S LIKE TO HAVE YOUR BRAIN TRANSPLANTED INTO A METAL BODY? IT'S LIFE IMPRISONMENT!

CAN YOU IMAGINE HOW CRUDE ROBOT SENSES ARE, COMPARED TO HUMAN ONES, HUH? ALL I HAVE ARE MEMORIES OF THE WAY THINGS USED TO FEEL OR TASTE.

YOU KNOW, THEY SAY THAT AMPUTEES FEEL PHANTOM PAINS WHERE THEIR LIMBS USED TO BE. WELL, I'M A TOTAL AMPUTEE.

I'M HAUNTED BY THE GHOST OF MY ENTIRE BODY! I GET HEADACHES, YOU KNOW, AND I WANT TO CRAP UNTIL I REALIZE I DON'T HAVE ANY BOWELS.

AND...WHEN I LOOK AT A WOMAN, SOMETIMES I...

BUT SURELY THE DOOM PATROL HELPED TO...

THE DOOM PATROL? DON'T TALK TO ME...IT... THE DOOM PATROL KILLS PEOPLE. IT CHEWS THEM UP AND VOMITS OUT THE BITS.

IT KILLED RITA AND ARANI AND SCOTT...

CLIFF...

I JUST CAN'T STAND ANYMORE... I CAN'T GET THROUGH IT... REALLY...

I CAN'T.

22

23

...BUT YOU'VE NEVER *SPOKEN* BEFORE, I DON'T UNDERSTAND...

ALAMANCE MEMORIAL HOSPITAL

PER HAPSIHAD NOTHINGTO SAYLAR RY

IVELIVEDA BLACKBLACK DREAMOFSILENCE FORSOLONG

IMAWAKE NOWWIDE AWAKE

WHAT DO YOU WANT? I MEAN...

TOCONTINUE TOPERPETUATE TOGENERATE

YOURENOTSO CLEVERLARRY YOUTHINKIMUNA WAREYOUPRESSED THEALARM

IMADE YOUDOIT

WHAT?

INEEDTHE WOMANHERE

ITSNECES SARYFORMY PURPOSE

PURPOSE? WHAT PURPOSE?

YOUKNOW LARRYTHE UNIONTHE FUSION

THEALCHEMICAL MARRIAGE

NO.

24

TAKEMY
HANDNOW

NO...I...

OH, NO, PLEASE...
DON'T DO THIS
TO ME...

PLEASE...
WAIT...I...

TAKEMY
HANDLARRY

ITSTIMETOGO

LARRY?

LARRY,
WHAT'S HAP-
PENING?

ARE
YOU IN
THERE
?

HELLODOCTORPOOLE

WEVEBEEN
WAITINGFOR
YOU

TAKEMYHAND

25

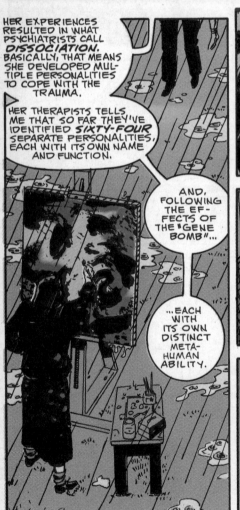

WHAT DO *NORMAL* PEOPLE HAVE IN THEIR LIVES?

WHAT?

WHAT DO *NORMAL* PEOPLE HAVE?

YOU'RE ASKING THE WRONG PERSON.

I'VE TRIED TO BE LIKE THEM, I *REALLY* HAVE.

BUT WHAT HAPPENS WHEN YOU JUST CAN'T BE STRONG ANY-MORE? WHAT HAPPENS IF YOU'RE *WEAK*?

MY PAINTING'S *RUINED.*

EVERY-THING'S *GONE* WRONG.

COME IN OUT OF THE RAIN.

30

I'M NOT ASHAMED TO SAY IT, MAN—I THREW UP RIGHT THERE ON THE SIDEWALK.

YOU EVER SMELL SKIN BURNING?

AND THIS IS THE BOOK?

SURE IS. GOD ALONE KNOWS WHAT THE THING'S MADE OF.

BLACK PAGES, MAN. WEIRD.

YOUR HELP'S BEEN APPRECIATED, OFFICER.

WE'LL BE IN TOUCH.

MY PLEASURE, PAL.

I DON'T KNOW WHY I EVER GOT INTO INTELLIGENCE. THIS "MAN IN BLACK" STUFF'S REALLY GETTING ME DOWN.

HOW D'YOU MANAGE TO KEEP UP THE ACT.

IT'S NOT AN ACT.

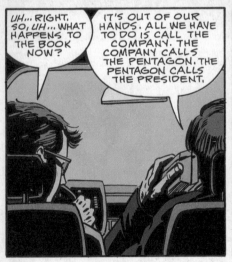

UH... RIGHT. SO, UH... WHAT HAPPENS TO THE BOOK NOW?

IT'S OUT OF OUR HANDS. ALL WE HAVE TO DO IS CALL THE COMPANY. THE COMPANY CALLS THE PENTAGON. THE PENTAGON CALLS THE PRESIDENT.

AND HE CALLS NILES CAULDER.

32

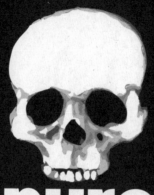

"I am nothing special, nothing **pure.** I am mud and flame."

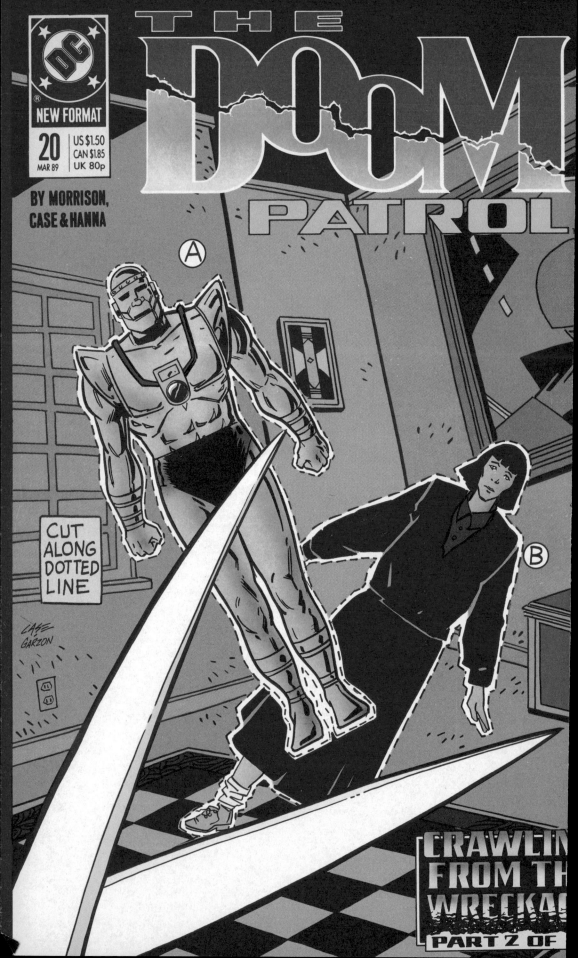

MACKEREL.
HERRING.
SEA BASS.

PIKE.
STURGEON.
TENCH.

PLAICE.
SALMON.

FROM A
CLEAR
SKY.

TROUT.

NO COD.

36

...YOU SAY THIS ALL HAPPENED LAST NIGHT?

ALAMANCE MEMORIAL HOSPITAL

THAT'S RIGHT.

THE TWO ORDERLIES WHO FOUND THE CREATURE ARE BEING TREATED FOR MINOR BURNS.

"*CREATURE*"? I THOUGHT WE WERE TALKING ABOUT *LARRY TRAINOR* HERE...

IT MAY HAVE BEEN LARRY TRAINOR LAST NIGHT, MR. CLAY, BUT IT'S CERTAINLY NOT LARRY TRAINOR NOW.

YOU SAY IT HAS BOTH MALE *AND* FEMALE PHYSICAL CHARACTER-ISTICS?

THAT'S IT EXACTLY, YES.

WE THINK...WE BELIEVE THAT THE CREATURE IS SOME KIND OF *AMALGA-MATION* OF MR. TRAINOR AND DOCTOR ELEANOR POOLE.

YOU'LL SEE THAT IT'S ALSO EMITTING SOME KIND OF RADIATION. WE HAD TO USE TREATED BANDAGES TO...

WELL, ANYWAY...

TRAINOR
E. POOLE

SEE FOR YOURSELF.

LARRY?

LARRY, DO YOU *KNOW* ME?

"NOTHING PURE...

"MY RACE IS MIXED, MY SEX IS MIXED, I AM WOMAN AND MAN AND LIGHT WITH DARKNESS, MIXED. *MIXED.*

"I AM NOTHING SPECIAL, NOTHING PURE.

"I AM MUD AND FLAME."

I *SEE.*

41

NOT LARRY NOR YET ELEANOR... I...

CAN YOU TELL US, LARRY?

CAN YOU TELL US WHAT HAPPENED?

REBIS.

CALL US REBIS.

AH.

WE'RE TIRED NOW. PLEASE LEAVE.

I CAN'T BELIEVE THIS. IT'S LIKE A NIGHTMARE. POOR LARRY...

THAT NAME HE SAID...

REBIS, IT WAS A TERM USED BY THE MEDIEVAL ALCHEMISTS TO IDENTIFY THE RESULT OF A CHYMICAL WEDDING.

YOU SHOULD READ MORE, JOSHUA.

WHATEVER IT IS, THE WHOLE THING'S A GROTESQUE TRAGEDY.

YES.

ONE MOMENT PLEASE, GENTLEMEN.

REBIS?

YES?

HOW WOULD YOU LIKE TO JOIN THE DOOM PATROL?

43

YOU'RE MAKING **PROGRESS**, CLIFF. THERE'S NO DENYING THAT.

WHAT DO YOU WANT, **MAGNUS**, A **MEDAL**?

I'M NOT TRYING TO TAKE ANY CREDIT FOR YOUR IMPROVEMENT. I THINK YOU DID THAT YOUR-SELF.

I'M TOLD YOU'VE BEEN SPENDING A LOT OF TIME WITH **CRAZY JANE.** HER THERAPIST SAYS YOUR HELP'S BEEN INVALUABLE.

WHAT DO YOU MAKE OF HER? JANE, I MEAN.

I DON'T KNOW. I'D NEVER EVEN **HEARD** OF A MULTIPLE PERSONALITY CASE LIKE HERS BEFORE.

SOMETIMES SHE CAN BE SIX OR SEVEN DIF-FERENT PEOPLE IN ONE CON-VERSA-TION.

I'M JUST TRYING TO HELP HER **ORGANIZE** HERSELF AND START CATALOGUING THE NEW SUPER-POWERS SHE'S BEEN SADDLED WITH.

KEEPS ME OFF THE STREETS, YOU KNOW?

YEAH, I KNOW.

LISTEN, CLIFF... ONE LAST THING...

44

...ND OF TOOK
D HEART WHEN
COMPLAINED
UT THE
UDITY OF
R ROBOT
BODY...

...ESPECIALLY WHEN YOU THINK OF THE WAY CYBERNETICS TECHNOLOGY HAS *IMPROVED* RECENTLY.

YOU MADE ME *THINK*, CLIFF.

SO... AH... I'M GOING TO BUILD YOU A *NEW* BODY.

I'LL BE IN TOUCH, OKAY?

HA.

CLIFF?

OH, HI THERE, JANE.

TALK OF THE DEVIL, HUH?

DRIVER 8. WE HAVEN'T MET YET.

WHAT? ...OH... SURE.

HOW YOU DOING?

IT'S NOT EASY KEEPING TRACK OF ALL YOUR PERSONALITIES.

WE'RE NOT PERSONALITIES, WE'RE *PERSONS*.

CAN WE WALK AWHILE?

SEE, I DRIVE THE *TRAIN*, AND...

HOLD ON, YOU'RE WAY AHEAD OF ME. WHAT TRAIN'S THIS?

A.T. J...
CAR...

THE TRAIN OF *THOUGHT*, I MONITOR THE STATIONS OF THE *UNDERGROUND*.

THAT'S WHERE YOU ALL LIVE, RIGHT?...IN JANE'S HEAD...THE UNDERGROUND.

YOU'RE OVER-SIMPLIFYING, BUT YES, THAT'S ABOUT RIGHT.

ANYWAY, SOME OF THE OTHERS HAVE ASKED ME TO TELL YOU THAT... WELL, THAT THEY *LIKE* YOU.

RAIN BRAIN SAYS YOUR VOICE IS LIKE AN OLD BLACK TELE-PHONE AND *BLACK ANNIS* TOLD ME TO TELL YOU THAT YOU'RE THE FIRST MAN SHE HASN'T WANTED TO *CASTRATE*.

TELL HER SHE'D BE TOO LATE ANYWAY.

OH, AND *BABY DOLL* LIKES YOUR *NAME*: SHE CALLS YOU "SHELTERING CLIFF" NOW. SHE'S ALWAYS BEEN REALLY EMBARRASSING LIKE THAT.

I THINK YOU'RE OKAY, TOO.

YEAH, IT'S GOT TO BE SAID...

IN **STUTTGART**, ALL THE CLOCKS CHIME FIFTEEN.

SIMULTANEOUSLY.

IN **KYOTO**, FOUR STAINLESS STEEL PYRAMIDS ARE FOUND ROTATING FIVE FEET ABOVE GROUND.

IN **PATAGONIA**, A LIBRARY IS DISCOVERED. THE BOOKS IT CONTAINS ARE UNKNOWN, UNREADABLE.

IN **JOHANNESBURG**, A LITTLE GIRL NAMED HARRIET INEXPLICABLY CATCHES FIRE.

IN **REYKJAVIK**, THREE SHADOWS COME TO LIFE AND MURDER THEIR OWNERS.

IN **LONDON**, MADAME TUSSAUD'S WAX FIGURE OF **JOHN LENNON** BEGINS TO BLEED FROM BULLET WOUND STIGMATA.

JOHN WINSTON ONO LENNON 1940-1980

IN **ROME**, IN **LENINGRAD**, IN **DARWIN**.

"THE DOOR FLEW OPEN, IN HE RAN,

"THE GREAT, LONG, RED-LEGGED SCISSOR-MAN."

mindless violence.

"I couldn't think of one clever way to stop this guy, so I just trusted to

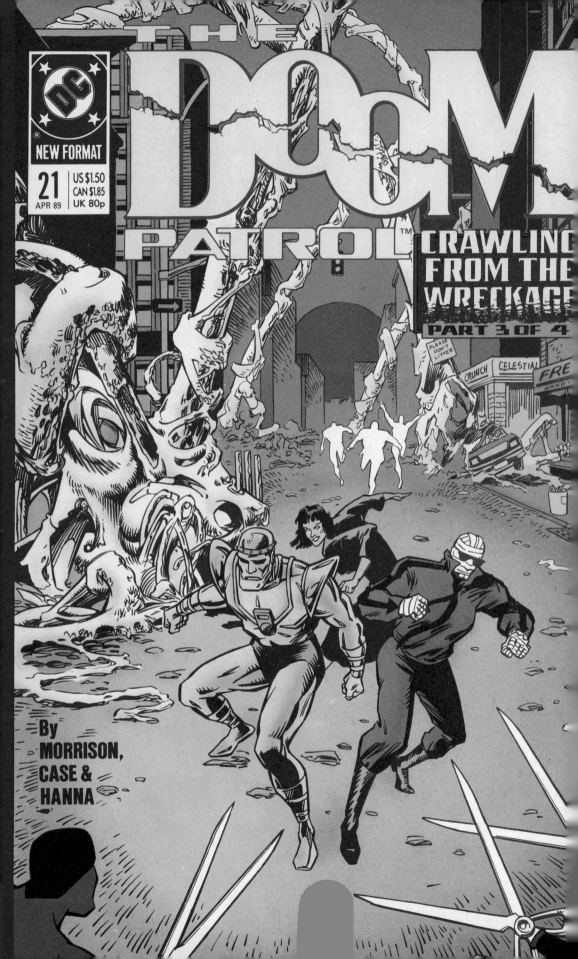

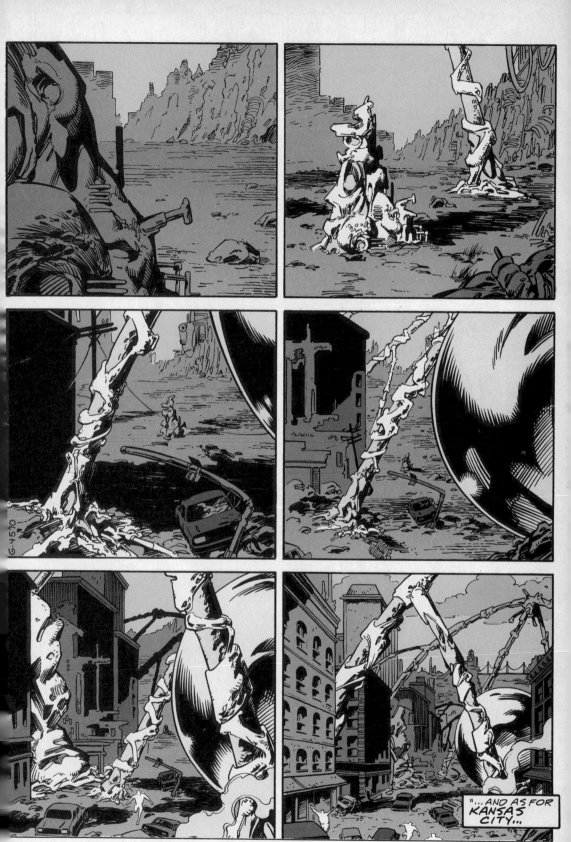

"...AND AS FOR KANSAS CITY..."

"AT FIRST, EVERYTHING WAS DEAD QUIET, LIKE A GRAVEYARD.

"AND THEN I HEARD WHISPERING."

SCISSORMEN!

DEFEATING BREADFRUIT IN ADUMBRATE.

CRASHLAND, FOR AWARD PRIMATE.

YUCCA OR PRIORITY?

LEMUR NEVER HIBERNATES.

"I WAS BEGINNING TO WONDER HOW MUCH LONGER WE COULD EXPECT TO BE LUCKY."

"IT TOOK US AN HOUR AND A HALF TO FIND UNION STATION."

WELCOME TO DOOM PATROL HEAD-QUARTERS.

YOU CAN SEE WE ALWAYS TRY TO MAKE VISITORS FEEL AT HOME.

AH, I SHOULD HAVE GUESSED THERE'D BE NO ONE HERE.

I SAID IT MYSELF, THE DOOM PATROL'S DEAD.

I DON'T KNOW WHAT I WAS EXPECTING, MAYBE JUST A...

CLIFF.

RHODE ISLAND?

"AND THEN OUR LUCK RAN OUT."

CLIFF!

KABWHOON KAP

DOTE OVER GANTRIES!

"WE WERE UP THE CREEK THIS TIME, THAT WAS FOR SURE. AND YOU KNOW ME; I'M NOT A SOPHISTICATED KIND OF GUY."

GET BACK.

GET BACK!

"I COULDN'T THINK OF ONE CLEVER WAY TO STOP THIS GUY, SO I JUST TRUSTED TO MINDLESS VIOLENCE."

UNNGH!

"AND I FLATTENED THE UGLY BASTARD."

BAWHOOM!

NOW MOVE IT!

BOP

BA-TOOM BA-TOOM BA-TOOM

"WE MADE FOR THE SUB-BASEMENT.

"NOW I DID HAVE A PLAN.

AND ALL I NEEDED WAS A PLANE."

EXIT

HERE! THIS ONE'S FINE!

CLIFF! ANOTHER SCISSOR-MAN!

JUST GIVE ME A SECOND! I...

"AND THEN SOMETHING *WEIRD* HAPPENED."

JANE?

JANE, ARE YOU...

OH MY GOD.

THERE *IS* NO GOD.

I KILLED HIM.

"IT WAS THE FIRST TIME I'D SEEN ONE OF JANE'S PERSONALITIES ACTUALLY PHYSICALLY TRANSFORM HER BODY.

"I'M TELLING YOU, IT WAS THE SCARIEST THING I'D SEEN ALL NIGHT.

"AND I GUESS THE SCISSORMAN THOUGHT SO, TOO.

"SHE TOOK HIM APART."

"ALL I CAN REMEMBER THINKING IS 'NO *BLOOD*. THERE'S NO *BLOOD*.'"

"AND THEN IT WAS ALL OVER.

"IT TOOK *SECONDS*."

NOTHING!

SCARLET RIBBONS!

EMPTY CLOTHES!

AAAAA

JANE!

HAS SHE GONE? *BLACK ANNIS?* HAS SHE GONE? HAS SHE GONE?

IT'S *OKAY*. YOU DID GOOD.

NOW, COME ON...

IT REALLY IS TIME WE WERE OUT OF HERE.

"WE HAULED OURSELVES UP INTO THAT JET LIKE OUR TAILS WERE ON FIRE."

I JUST HOPE I CAN REMEMBER HOW TO FLY THIS THING.

RIGHT.

FFWASHOM

AND THAT'S IT, UNTIL WE ARRIVED *HERE.*

IT'S A NICE PLACE. VERY *MODEST.*

IT BELONGED TO THE ORIGINAL *JUSTICE LEAGUE OF AMERICA.* THE GOVERNMENT WANTED TO USE IT TO STORE NUCLEAR WASTE, BUT I PERSUADED THEM TO GIVE IT TO ME.

ANYWAY, THAT'S BESIDE THE POINT. IT'S GOOD TO HAVE YOU BACK, CLIFF.

NOW, HOW DO WE PROPOSE TO DEAL WITH THE CURRENT CRISIS?

IF WE HAD ANY *SENSE,* WE'D CALL *SUPERMAN.*

WE DON'T *NEED* SUPERMAN. WE HAVE A MAJOR CLUE IN THE *BLACK BOOK* THAT WAS PASSED ON TO ME BY THE INTELLIGENCE SERVICES.

A MAN DIED IN FLAMES, CLUTCHING THAT BOOK.

I'VE FINISHED.

THE LAST WORD HE SAID WAS *"SCISSOR-MEN."*

NOW, IF YOUR FRIEND IS AS GOOD AS YOU SAY SHE IS, WE MAY BE ABLE TO START *DECIPHERING* THE BOOK OVER THE NEXT TWENTY-FOUR HOURS...

EXCUSE ME.

I'VE *FINISHED.*

"ORQWITH IS A CITY OF **MIRACLES**. A CITY OF GLASS LABYRINTHS AND OBSERVATORIES MADE OF BONE.

"ACCORDING TO THE BLACK BOOK, **OUR** REALITY IS JUST A PALE **SHADOW** OF 'THE SPLENDOR OF ORQWITH.'

"THE CITY GROWS BY IMPLANTING PARTS OF ITS OWN REALITY INTO THAT OF OTHER WORLDS, YOU SEE. IT INFILTRATES THEM, BIT-BY-BIT.

"FIRST IN **SMALL** WAYS, THEN IN CATASTROPHIC FASHION.

"UNTIL FINALLY IT **ENGULFS** THEM.

"AND THEY **BECOME** ORQWITH."

YEAH, BUT IS THIS A **BOOK** OR IS IT **REAL**?

WHAT'S SUPPOSED TO HAVE HAPPENED TO THESE PHILOSOPHER-GUYS? IN THE **BOOK**, I MEAN?

IN THE END, THEY'RE **DEVOURED** BY THEIR OWN CREATION.

"THE BOOK BECOMES THE GATEWAY BETWEEN THE IMAGINARY AND THE REAL.

"AND ORQWITH GETS **OUT**.

THE POSTSCRIPT READS SOMETHING LIKE, "AND THE BOOK THEY CREATED IS CALLED 'THE BOOK WITH NO TITLE.'"

THAT'S THE NAME OF THIS BOOK.

THIS IS WAY BEYOND ME.

SO EVERYTHING IN THE BOOK IS ACTUALLY HAPPENING IN REAL LIFE.

HOW CAN THAT BE POSSIBLE?

I DON'T KNOW! I'M ONLY TELLING YOU WHAT MAMA PENTECOST SAID, THAT'S ALL!

WHAT ABOUT THE SCISSOR-MEN?

APPARENTLY, THEY'RE SOME KIND OF RELIGIOUS SECT. THEY WORSHIP A GOD WHO EXISTS AT A MYTHICAL CROSSROADS WHERE REALITIES MEET.

IT'S A KIND OF PARADOX, I GUESS.

THE PHILOSOPHERS IMAGINED THEM TO BE ORQWITH'S ANSWER TO THE INQUISITION.

I THINK THEY JUST BASED THEM ON THE BOGEYMAN FROM HEINRICH HOFFMAN'S "STRUWWELPETER."

OH, TERRIFIC!

ARE THEY REAL OR AREN'T THEY?

THEY'RE BOTH. DON'T YOU SEE, IT'S...

CLIFF...

KLIK

7

WHY DON'T YOU JUDGE FOR YOURSELF?

MY GOD.

WE RAN INTO IT LAST NIGHT AND, AS YOU SEE, *REB* MANAGED TO RESTRAIN IT.

HELLO, CLIFF.

LARRY...?

THE LEACHING WILL BE NOVELISTIC FOR EFFACEMENT!

CURDLE YOUR PILGRIMAGE

CURDLE YOUR PILGRIMAGE!

WHAT'S HE SAYING?

HOW THE HELL SHOULD I KNOW? WHAT AM I, AN *EXPERT*?

EXCUSE ME FOR LIVING!

OH, JUST IGNORE *HER*, CLIFF!

HAMMER-HEAD'S ALWAYS LIKE THAT.

ALL I WANT IS THE ANSWER TO ONE SIMPLE QUESTION BEFORE I RUN SCREAMING BACK TO THE *BUG-HOUSE*:

IS THIS *REAL* OR ISN'T IT?

REALITY AND UNREALITY HAVE NO CLEAR DIS-TINCTION IN OUR PRESENT CIRCUMSTANCES, CLIFF.

IT MIGHT HELP TO CONSIDER THE ZEN *KOAN,* "FIRST THERE IS A MOUNTAIN, THEN THERE IS NO MOUNTAIN, THEN THERE IS."

SURE. THAT'S *REALLY* HELPED TO CLEAR THINGS UP.

SO WHAT NOW?

JUST TELL ME AND I'LL GO ALONG WITH IT.

FIRST, I WANT TO FIND OUT JUST HOW EXTENSIVE THE INTRUSION OF ORQWITH HAS BEEN SO FAR AND *THEN* I WANT TO TRACK DOWN THE "PHILOSOPHERS" WHO COMPILED THE BLACK BOOK.

AND WHAT DO I DO?

YOU KEEP A CLOSE EYE ON *THAT.*

CLIFF! WHAT'S HAPPENING?

THEY GOT HIM.

ONE MINUTE HE WAS HERE...

HE WAS RIGHT HERE AND THEN...

INTERESTING.

"INTERESTING?"

WHAT ABOUT JOSH?

THEY'RE OUT THERE.

WHAT?

I CAN *FEEL* THEM.

A STRANGE MASS *ABSENCE* OF BEING.

THEY'RE *OUT* THERE.

WAITING FOR US!

"FIRST THERE IS A MOUNTAIN.

"THEN THERE IS NO MOUNTAIN.

"THEN THERE IS."

"why is there something instead of nothing?"

Beyond the Ossuary, the half-life of the city continues. Sleepwalkers drift among marvels wrought in the bone of the unnumbered dead.

Empty orbits contain electric bulbs that light and go dim in response to changes in air pressure or humidity.

RAY'S

Here, the skull of a consumptive child becomes part of a great machine for calculating the motions of the stars.

Here, a yellow bird frets within the ribcage of an unjust man.

SIMPLE KNUCKLES INC.

Around every corner is some fresh wonder: the weeping clock, the water gardens, the hymning birds, the mechanical orchards.

Yet, no matter how strange, no matter how beautiful, everything in Orqwith is dulled by the taint of long familiarity.

When you see it, you will know it.

For all of us, in the end, come to the City of Bone.

And what was once a place of dreams is now only real.

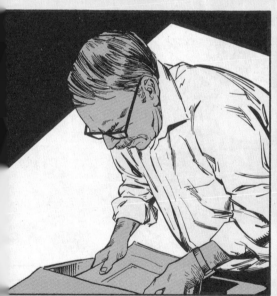

FAWHOOM

AH, REINMANN, I PRESUME.

MAY I COME IN?

MY GOD... YOU CAN'T JUST...

MY GOVERNMENT CONTACTS TRACKED YOU DOWN VIA A *FRIEND* OF YOURS --HE DIED IN A CAR ACCIDENT A FEW DAYS AGO.

I WANT TO TALK ABOUT THE *BLACK BOOK* HE WAS CARRYING.

I WANT TO TALK ABOUT *ORQWITH.*

I'M NOT AFRAID OF YOU!

YOU THINK I'M AFRAID OF A *CRIPPLE?* YOU THINK I...

BLAM

AAAAA

LOOKS LIKE *YOU'RE* A CRIPPLE, TOO.

NOW.

SHALL WE TALK?

IT'S ONLY A FLESH WOUND, REINMANN.

STOP *WHIMPERING* AND GO ON WITH WHAT YOU WERE SAYING. YOU WERE TALKING ABOUT THE *BOOK*...

IT WAS A *GAME* REALLY, JUST AN INTELLECTUAL JOKE. WE GOT TOGETHER AND CREATED *ORQWITH*— ITS LANGUAGE, ITS RELIGION... YOU KNOW...

AND THEN SOMEHOW ORQWITH ...CROSSED OVER. THE SCISSORMEN TOOK *POLLOCK* FIRST, THEN *SCHRADER* TRIED TO DESTROY THE *BOOK*...

IT'S TOO LATE NOW. OUR FICTION'S EATING INTO THE REAL WORLD. SOON THE WHOLE WORLD WILL *BE* ORQWITH...

PLEASE... MY LEG... IT'S...

HOW DO WE *STOP* ORQWITH?

OH, FOR GOD'S SAKE, I DON'T KNOW! IT SHOULDN'T EVEN EXIST AT ALL!

WE...WE BUILT A LOGICAL INCONSISTENCY INTO THE FICTION, A BASIC *CONTRADICTION,* UPON WHICH THE ENTIRE WORLD IS FOUNDED.

IT'S THE FUNDAMENTAL PROBLEM OF PHILOSOPHY— "WHY IS THERE *SOME-THING* INSTEAD OF *NOTHING?*" THE MOST BASIC OF ALL QUESTIONS.

ORQWITH *CAN* BE DESTROYED.

IT JUST HAS TO BE MADE TO *CONFRONT* ITS OWN UNREALITY, THAT'S ALL.

HAH! THAT'S ALL...

...THAT' ALL...

...SO THE PRIEST WHO KNEW THE ANSWER WAS A *LIAR*, YOU SEE, WHICH MEANT THAT HIS ANSWER TO THE QUESTION MUST *ALSO* HAVE BEEN A LIE.

HE SAID "THERE IS SOMETHING INSTEAD OF NOTHING," SINCE THAT WAS A LIE, THEN WHAT HE WAS *REALLY* SAYING IS THAT THERE *WASN'T* SOMETHING INSTEAD OF NOTHING.

THAT'S WHEN ORQWITH COLLAPSED.

I *THINK* THAT'S HOW IT HAPPENED, ANYWAY.

WELL, YOU'LL BE GLAD TO KNOW THAT THE WORLD-WIDE ANOMALOUS ACTIVITY CAUSED BY THE INTRUSION OF ORQWITH HAS NOW APPARENTLY *CEASED*.

WE WERE LUCKY THAT THE WHOLE CRISIS WAS MAN-MADE AND FOUNDED ON *HUMAN* LOGICAL PROCESSES.

...W ABOUT ...U, JOSHUA? ...W ARE YOU ...LING AFTER ...UR ORDEAL?

IT WAS LIKE A *DREAM*. I KEEP FLASHING ON IMAGES AND FEELINGS, BUT I DON'T REALLY REMEMBER *WHAT* HAPPENED AFTER I WAS SNATCHED AWAY THIS MORNING.

JUST AS WELL, I GUESS.

SO THEY ALL LIVED HAPPILY EVER AFTER, HUH?

OR DO I GET THE FEELING YOU WANT TO *SAY* SOMETHING, CHIEF?

YES, YES, CLIFF, I *DO* WANT TO SAY SOMETHING.

I THINK IT'S CLEAR FROM WHAT'S HAPPENED OVER THE PAST FEW DAYS THAT THE WORLD NEEDS THE DOOM PATROL...

...NEEDS *US* MORE THAN EVER.

DON'T YOU SEE? THERE ARE AREAS IN WHICH ONLY *WE* ARE QUALIFIED TO OPERATE. WHEN THE RATIONAL WORLD BREAKS DOWN, WE CAN *COPE*...

...BECAUSE WE'VE *BEEN* THERE, IN OURSELVES.

WE HAVE *KNOWN* MADNESS...

...AND DELIRIUM...

...AND WE ARE NO LONGER *AFRAID.*

THE WORLD HAS TURNED ITS BACK ON US, BUT IT'S TIME TO STOP BEING *VICTIMS*, TIME TO SHOW THEM WE'RE MORE THAN JUST "FREAKS," MORE THAN JUST "CRIPPLES." BELIEVE ME, THEY *NEED* US.

AND WE NEED EACH *OTHER.*

DON'T LET THE DOOM PATROL DIE AGAIN.

JOIN ME.

PLEASE.

AH, WHAT THE HELL!

ANYTHING TO AVOID A QUIET LIFE.

GOOD

EPILOGUE

FADE UP HOSPITAL ACOUSTIC: ECHOING WHISPERS IN LONG, OVERLIT CORRIDORS. LIFE SUPPORT MACHINERY, MARKING TIME.

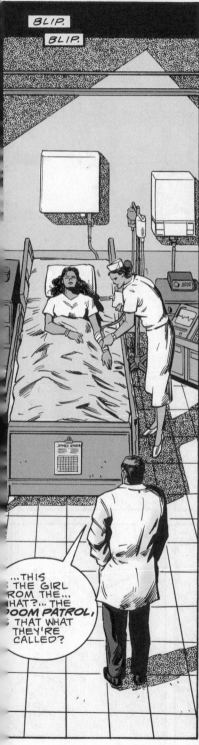

BLIP.

BLIP.

...THIS IS THE GIRL FROM THE... WHAT?... THE DOOM PATROL, IS THAT WHAT THEY'RE CALLED?

RHEA JONES, THAT'S RIGHT. THERE'S BEEN NO CHANGE IN HER CONDITION, I'M AFRAID.

IT MAKES ME SO ANGRY... THE WAY THESE PEOPLE JUST THROW THEMSELVES INTO DANGEROUS SITUATIONS AND THEN EXPECT US TO...

AH, WHAT'S THE USE?

SUPER-HEROES. THEY MAKE ME SICK!

RHEA.

107

MY SLEEPING BEAUTY.

BLIP.

BLIP.

FADE.

EPILOGUE 2

IN PARAGUAY, THE SEASON OF RAINS HAS ARRIVED.

DOCTOR BRUCKNER!

AHHHH

DOCTOR?

DOCTOR BRUCKNER?

LIE STILL!

I'LL GET HELP!

...HAH...

WHAT?

...HAH-HAH-HERR NIEMANO...

...HERR NIEMANO!...

...OUT...

HE GOT OUT!

LOOK!

HE GOT OUT!

"Sorry about the writing. Robot fingers, you

know."

RHODE ISLAND. DOOM PATROL HEADQUARTERS.

THE WIND FROM THE EAST.

GOOD MORNING, JOSHUA.

UNSEASONABLY *COLD*, DON'T YOU THINK? THE TEMPERATURE DROPPED DRAMATICALLY...

...AT A QUARTER AFTER THREE LAST NIGHT.

YEAH.

WHAT *IS* THAT?

IT'S WHAT WE CALL THE *LORENZ ATTRACTOR*--A COMPUTER IMAGE OF THE INFINITE HIDDEN STRUCTURE CONTAINED IN A CHAOTIC STREAM OF DATA.

A PICTURE OF THE RULES THAT GOVERN *WEATHER*, FOR INSTANCE.

I'LL TAKE YOUR WORD FOR IT.

WEATHER IS COMPLETELY *UNPREDICTABLE*, YOU SEE. THEORETICALLY, A CATASTROPHIC CYCLONE IN *BANGLADESH* CAN BE TRACED BACK TO SOMETHING AS SIMPLE AS THE TINY PERTURBATIONS MADE IN THE AIR BY THE WING OF A *BUTTERFLY* IN SOUTH AMERICA.

IT'S A CHAIN REACTION OF EVENT AND CONSEQUENCE THAT...

YEAH, LISTEN, IT'S NOT THAT I DON'T WANT TO TALK *METEOROLOGY* WITH YOU OR ANYTHING, BUT I REALLY CAME UP TO TELL YOU THAT I'D...WELL, I'D LIKE TO *ACCEPT* YOUR OFFER.

I'D LIKE TO STAY WITH THE *DOOM PATROL*.

114

FINE.

THAT'S UNDER THE TERMS WE AGREED; I'M WITH THE TEAM PURELY IN A *MEDICAL* CAPACITY.

NO MORE SUPER-HERO STUFF.

OKAY?

FINE. I SAID "FINE," *JOSHUA.*

YOUR EXPERTISE WILL BE MOST WELCOME.

I THINK IT'S ESSENTIAL THAT THE DOOM PATROL HAS SOME GOOD, SOLID IN-HOUSE BACK-UP.

AND NOW I'D LIKE YOU TO MEET THE *SECOND* MEMBER OF WHAT I'VE COME TO THINK OF AS THE "OUTER TEAM."

SHE ARRIVED TEN MINUTES AGO.

I BELIEVE YOU ALREADY KNOW *DOROTHY SPINNER.*

...HI...

115

117

...SO WHAT DO YOU THINK OF THE NEW DOOM PATROL HEADQUARTERS, DOROTHY?

PRETTY SMART, HUH?

I DIDN'T SEE THE *OLD* ONE, MR. CLAY.

NO...NO, I GUESS YOU DIDN'T ...SO, WHAT BRINGS YOU OUT HERE, ANYWAY?

WELL, IT WAS *PROFESSOR CAULDER*, I GUESS. HE CALLED MY DAD AFTER THE *INVASION* AND ALL.

HE MUST HAVE HEARD ABOUT WHAT *HAPPENED* TO ME WHEN THE GENE BOMB WENT OFF.

YEAH? SO WHAT DID HAPPEN?

OH... WELL, IT WAS KIND OF...

WAIT A MINUTE!

I'M SORRY, DOROTHY, BUT IS IT JUST MY *EARS* OR DO YOU HEAR SOMETHING? KIND OF LIKE SQUISHY...

...FOOT-STEPS...

OH MY GOD.

...WE WERE GOING TO GET *MARRIED,* TWO MONTHS TIME.

YOU'RE TAKING ME APART, ELEANOR...

REBIS. NOT ELEANOR.

LISTEN, JUST GO, WILL YOU?

PLEASE JUST...

OH, GOD, ELEANOR.

I DON'T...

WHAT AM I GOING TO *DO?*

WHAT AM I GOING TO DO?

DON'T GET BLOOD ON THE COAT.

121

...IT'S THE *DOOM PATROL*, OKAY? HERE'S THE ADDRESS. WE'LL TAKE CARE OF THE DAMAGE.

SORRY ABOUT THE WRITING. ROBOT FINGERS, YOU KNOW?

AND REMEMBER, KIDS: DON'T WALK THROUGH PLATE GLASS WINDOWS!

JANE!

JANE! WAIT!

KREE

HONK!

HONK!

12 14 15 16

JANE!

Ding

DAMN!

Phon

Phone

Phone

125

SCISSORS.

I NEED A PAIR OF SCISSORS.

...CHIEF?...YEAH, LISTEN...SOMETHING WEIRD'S HAPPENED DOWN AT THE HOSPITAL...

YEAH.. RHEA'S VANISHE ...POSSIBL ABDUCTE

RANDOM WORDS. CUT PHRASES.

IT'S A KIND OF DIVINATION, LIKE CASTING THE RUNES OR READING THE FLIGHT OF BIRDS.

ONLY WITH WORDS.

SNIP SNIP

...AS SOON AS REBIS GETS BACK, SEND HIM DOWN HERE... YEAH...

I'VE GOT A FEELING ABOUT THIS ONE, CHIEF..

...YEAH... STRAIGHT AWAY...

SHUFFLE THEM.

SEE HOW THEY FALL? LIKE SNOW.

EXCUSE ME, ARE YOU WITH THAT WOMAN WHO...

DON'T WORRY ABOUT IT. SHE'S A SUPER-HERO.

THE MUSIC COMES IN WAVES.

FREAKBEAT VIVALDI SAMPLED AND SPLICED TOGETHER WITH THE SCREAMS OF MURDERED WOMEN AND BUTTER-FLIES.

AND WEDDING BELLS.

THE CLAMOR OF WEDDING BELLS.

PETALS?

YOU'RE LATE.

YOU'RE TOO LATE.

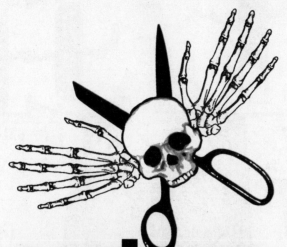

"You're a **curious** creature, aren't you? A thing of parts."

138

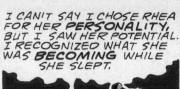

ANYWAY.

WHAT WAS I SAYING?

YES. YES...I'VE DECIDED TO *MARRY*. ALL WORK AND NO PLAY MAKES JACK A DULL BOY, AFTER ALL.

I CAN'T SAY I CHOSE RHEA FOR HER *PERSONALITY*, BUT I SAW HER POTENTIAL. I RECOGNIZED WHAT SHE WAS *BECOMING* WHILE SHE SLEPT.

AND LOOK AT THOSE *HIPS!*

THINK OF THE *CHILDREN* WE'LL HAVE.

HOW MANY TIMES MUST I TELL YOU?

HANDS

OFF!

AWWW SZZZH...

KAPOW

149

DETROIT. HOT SKIES. EMERGENCY SIRENS. FALLING GLASS. ALCOHOLIC SWEAT.

LLOYD JEFFERSON.

din do nuthin no way din do it

that ole place just come down bang! all on its own sure did me i din do nuthin i

PSSST!

LLOYD.

WUHH?

I DIN DO IT! REALLY I

IT'S ALL RIGHT, LLOYD. I SAW WHAT YOU DID.

I'M A FRIEND.

WHASSAT? I CAN'T SEE YOU STRAIGHT, MAN.

WHO'S THERE?

IT'S ME, LLOYD. I'M THE SAVIOR OF THE LOST AND DISPOSSESSED. THE PATRON SAINT OF INSIGNIFICANCE.

I'M MR. NOBODY.

AND I COME TO WELCOME YOU, TO SET YOU FREE.

IN THE NAME OF BROTHER-HOOD.

"You shot your imaginary friends? With what?"

"An imaginary gun! What else?"

BEFORE I GO, JOSHUA-- *MAXWELL LORD* OF THE *JUSTICE LEAGUE* CALLED YESTERDAY.

APPARENTLY A NUMBER OF ITEMS WERE LEFT BEHIND IN THE *SOUVENIR ROOM* WHEN THE ORIGINAL LEAGUE *ABANDONED* THIS COMPLEX.

LORD IS PARTICULARLY INTERESTED IN SOMETHING CALLED A *MATERIOPTIKON.*

A *WHAT?*

MATERIOPTIKON. AS FAR AS I UNDERSTAND, IT'S A DEVICE THAT *DOCTOR DESTINY* USED TO EXTERNALIZE THE SUBCONSCIOUS.

THE LEAGUE RECENTLY HAD SOME KIND OF TEDIOUS SKIRMISH WITH DESTINY...

...AND LORD IS ANXIOUS TO RETRIEVE ALL COPIES OF THE MATERIOPTIKON.

YOU WOULDN'T MIND TAKING A LOOK IN THE SOUVENIR ROOM, WOULD YOU?

...UM... MR. CLAY...

EXCUSE ME, MR. CLAY...

CONFESSIONS OF AN ENGLISH OPIUM EATER

DOROTHY! HI! HOW ARE YOU?

YOU SETTLING IN OKAY?

WELL, NOT REALLY. THERE'S SOMETHING WRONG WITH THE *TEEVEE.*

I DIDN'T REALLY WANT TO BOTHER YOU...

HEY, NO PROBLEM! I'M NOT TOO GREAT WITH TELEVISIONS, BUT I'LL TAKE A LOOK.

YEAH, WELL, IT GOT SO I DIDN'T *LIKE* THE STORIES THEY STARTED TO TELL ME.

THEY WERE GIVING ME BAD DREAMS.

THEY TOLD ME ABOUT THE LITTLE MERMAID AND ABOUT THE GIRL WHO COULDN'T STOP DANCING TILL THEY CUT OFF HER *FEET*...

SO I *SHOT* THEM.

YOU *SHOT* YOUR IMAGINARY FRIENDS?

WITH WHAT?

AN IMAGINARY *GUN!* WHAT ELSE?

I TOLD THEM I WANTED TO SHOW THEM SOMETHING. THEN I TOOK THEM 'ROUND BEHIND THE BARN AND I SHOT THEM.

WELL, I SUPPOSE THAT'S *ONE* WAY OF DOING IT...

WHAT *AGE* WERE YOU WHEN THIS HAPPENED?

ABOUT *ELEVEN,* I GUESS.

ELEVEN?

DOROTHY, LISTEN... THE CHIEF ASKED ME TO CHECK SOMETHING OUT AND I'D BETTER DO IT NOW BEFORE I *FORGET.*

CAN WE TALK AGAIN IN A COUPLE OF MINUTES?

SURE.

I'LL BE BACK AS QUICKLY AS I CAN.

DON'T GO AWAY!

MY GOD.

OKAY.

OKAY.

WE'D BETTER *TALK* ABOUT THIS, DOROTHY.

IS IT YOUR PSYCHIC POWER? IS THAT WHAT'S MAKING THESE THINGS HAPPEN? THE WAY YOU MADE THAT *MONSTER* APPEAR WHEN YOU ARRIVED TWO DAYS AGO?

DOROTHY, CAN YOU MAKE THESE THINGS GO AWAY, LIKE YOU DID WITH THE MONSTER?

I *CAN'T!*

I DIDN'T MAKE THIS HAPPEN, I DON'T HAVE POWER THAT *STRONG.*

177

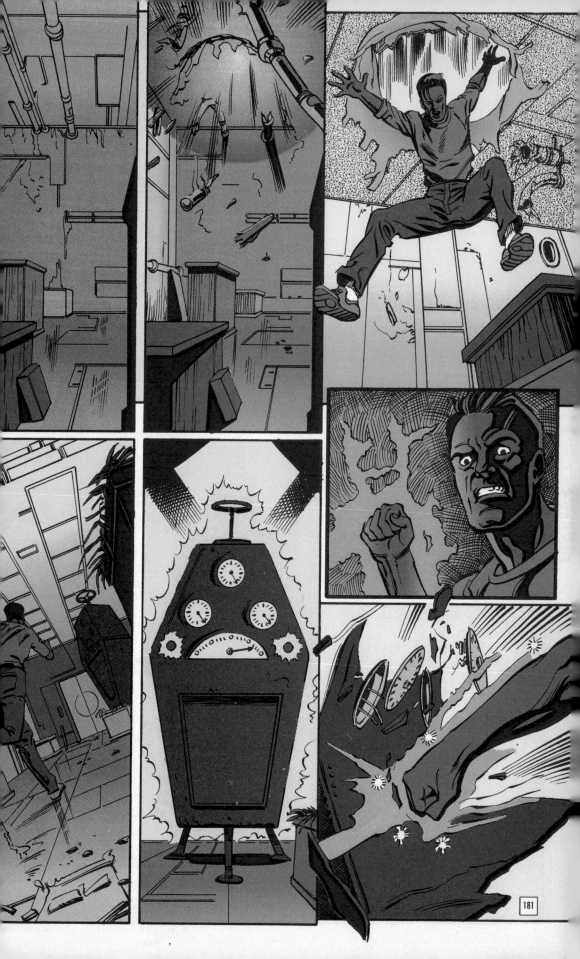

a word from the author.

(the **following letter** from

grant

morrison

originally appeared in

DOOM PATROL #20

I'll be perfectly honest with you right from the start and admit that I find it incredibly difficult to write this sort of thing. DOOM PATROL editor extraordinaire Bob Greenberger asked me to fill up a couple of pages by introducing myself to the readers of this magazine and waffling on about whatever came to mind. As far as I'm concerned, this pretty much gives me *carte blanche* to bore the pants off everyone by indulging in a series of childhood reminiscences and idle speculations, so, like I always say, "Get out now while you still can!"

Okay. Now that only the real diehards and the serious masochists are left, let's talk about the Doom Patrol.

My involvement with DOOM PATROL came about in the trembling spring of '88 when Bob called me and asked if I'd like to take over the scripting chores on the book, following the departure of Paul Kupperberg. Bob had seen the script for the ARKHAM ASYLUM book that I'm doing with Dave McKean, and he wondered if I could do to the members of the Doom Patrol what I'd done to Batman and the inmates of DC's infamous fictional loony bin.

I was busy with ANIMAL MAN and with my *Zenith* series for *2000 AD* and with all sorts of other things too numerous and too boring to mention, and I wasn't sure if I really wanted to take on another monthly book on top of all this stuff. The more I thought about it, however, the more attractive the idea of revamping the Doom Patrol began to look. What really clinched it was the fact that, when I was a kid, I hardly *ever* read DOOM PATROL; that comic *frightened* me, and the only reason I read any of the stories at all was that there was a certain dark and not-altogether-healthy glamour about those four characters.

That was good enough for me. I decided to write DOOM PATROL.

In these days of angst-ridden mutants and grittily realistic (yawn) urban vigilantes, the Doom Patrol no longer seem quite as extreme as they did back in 1963, but I'm sure that some of you reading this can still recall the genuine frisson that accompanied those early stories. Back in the '60s, when DC super-heroes still sported right-angled jawlines and Boy Scout principles, the Doom Patrol slouched into town like a pack of junkyard dogs with a grudge against mankind. Believe me, this team was *bad* news. An audience more accustomed to the freshly-laundered antics of Wayne Boring's Superman was suddenly confronted by a manic robot with a transplanted human brain, a bandaged pilot who was possessed by a mysterious Negative Being, and an ex-movie starlet whose life and career had been ruined by size-changing powers. To cap it all, this motley crew of complaining misfits was led by an irascible genius in a wheelchair. Add to that a cast of villains that included a disembodied brain and a talking French gorilla and you may begin to understand why those initial Doom Patrol adventures are still looked upon with such fondness by connoisseurs of the strange.

When I sat down to work out what I wanted to do with this book, I decided straight away that I would attempt to restore the sense of the bizarre that made the original Doom Patrol so memorable. I wanted to reconnect with the fundamental, radical concept of the book — that here was a team composed of *handicapped* people. These were no clean-limbed, wish-fulfillment super-adolescents who could model Calvins in their spare time. This was a group of people with serious physical problems and, perhaps, one too many bats in the belfry.

My feeling about the recent incarnation of the Doom Patrol was that, quite simply, they were too normal. I proposed that we create a more or less completely new team, based more clearly on the tight family structure of the original group. Paul Kupperberg, via the INVASION crossover, kindly agreed to kill or maim most of his characters and leave the field clear for me to introduce a Doom Patrol that was a little less comfortable, a little more unsettling, and, I hope, more faithful to the spirit of the Arnold Drake/Bruno Premiani stories of days gone by. Most of all, I wanted to break away from the massive influence that the Claremont/Byrne-era *X-Men* continue to exert over the whole concept of the comic book super-team and to forge a new style that would look forward to the '90s.

Sounds great on paper, doesn't it?

In the end, most of my ideas arrived like Hurricane Gilbert, in one wild week of constant and feverish inspiration. When it was over, I found myself with enough material to take me up to around issue #60, if we can possibly imagine ever getting that far. At which point — and since I'm rapidly running out of things to say — I'll waste some space by mentioning a few of the things that led to the creation of this new version of the Doom Patrol.

Most certainly a major influence was the work of Jan Svankmajer, whose films I saw while I was working on my Doom Patrol proposal. Svankmajer is a Czech filmmaker whose films are often mistakenly described as surrealist. (In truth, they're only surrealist in the strict "super real" sense of that much-maligned word.) The films are generally fairly short; they use a combination of live action and the animation of everyday objects; and they present a disturbing vision of a world set free from all logical constraints. Svankmajer has just released a full-length interpretation of *Alice's*

Adventures in Wonderland, and if you get the chance to see it, jump at it.

The season of Svankmajer films was augmented by "surrealist" classics like Kenneth Anger's *Eaux d'Artifice* and Maya Deren's eerie *Meshes of the Afternoon*, so when the time came to start work on DOOM PATROL, I'd immersed myself in the atmosphere of these weird, irrational worlds and was all set to bring some of that dream-like ambience to the stories I was planning.

Douglas Hofstadter's brilliant book *Gödel, Escher, Bach*, which is an immensely readable voyage into the twilight world of logic and abstract mathematics, was another useful springboard for me (as someone who rarely managed to get beyond writing my name on math exams, I'm doubly grateful to Hofstadter for being so perfectly lucid in his explanations) and some of that material will doubtless find its way into upcoming adventures.

When Rabbit Howls, the astonishing autobiography of multiple personality victim Truddi Chase, was another invaluable source of reference when it came to creating the Crazy Jane character. If you really want to have your mind blown, buy or steal that book and take a peek at what reality looks like from the other side.

Then there were the books on alchemy, the dreams I've used almost directly, the weird little stories told to me by friends and a million other things that I threw into the simmering stew that was the Doom Patrol proposal.

From here on in, we cast ourselves to the tender mercies of you, dear reader.

Anyway...

Basically, my aim is to bring back some of that ol' Doom Patrol magic by stripping the team down to its roots and returning, as quickly as possible, to the freewheeling weirdness that made the early stories so exhilarating. If things go as planned, we'll be hitting you with a rapid turnover of ideas and concepts and unusual villains. In fact, waiting just out of sight in the wings we have the Scissormen, we have Red Jack, we have Mr. Nobody and the New Brotherhood of Evil and, oh, all sorts of other groovy stuff!

I really can't think of anything else to say. I return the space to you, to fill with learned correspondence or Crayola™ squiggles. In taking my leave, I just want to grace you with one final thought:

Remember when all the other kids on the block had Superman and Batman as positive role models? Well, if you could only identify with a human brain in a metal body or a guy wrapped up in bandages, and if you grew up weird, welcome home. You're among friends now.

— grant morrison
dear old glasgow toon, scotland

1988

THE GRANT MORRISON LIBRARY

From VERTIGO. Suggested for mature readers.

ANIMAL MAN

A minor super-hero's consciousness is raised higher and higher until he becomes aware of his own fictitious nature in this revolutionary and existential series.

Volume 1: ANIMAL MAN
With Chas Truog, Doug Hazlewood and Tom Grummett

Volume 2: ORIGIN OF THE SPECIES
With Chas Truog, Doug Hazlewood and Tom Grummett

Volume 3: DEUS EX MACHINA
With Chas Truog, Doug Hazlewood and various

THE INVISIBLES

The saga of a terrifying conspiracy and the resistance movement combatting it — a secret underground of ultra-cool guerrilla cells trained in ontological and physical anarchy.

Volume 1: SAY YOU WANT A REVOLUTION
With Steve Yeowell and Jill Thompson

Volume 2: APOCALIPSTICK
With Jill Thompson, Chris Weston and various

Volume 3: ENTROPY IN THE U.K.
With Phil Jimenez, John Stokes and various

Volume 4: BLOODY HELL IN AMERICA
With Phil Jimenez and John Stokes

Volume 5: COUNTING TO NONE
With Phil Jimenez and John Stokes

Volume 6: KISSING MR. QUIMPER
With Chris Weston and various

Volume 7: THE INVISIBLE KINGDOM
With Philip Bond, Sean Phillips and various

SEAGUY
With Cameron Stewart

DOOM PATROL

The World's Strangest Heroes are reimagined even stranger and more otherworldly in this groundbreaking series exploring the mysteries of identity and madness.

Volume 1:
CRAWLING FROM THE WRECKAGE
With Richard Case, Doug Braithwaite, Scott Hanna, Carlos Garzon and John Nyberg

Volume 2:
THE PAINTING THAT ATE PARIS
With Richard Case and John Nyberg

THE FILTH
With Chris Weston and Gary Erskine

THE MYSTERY PLAY
With Jon J Muth

SEBASTIAN O
With Steve Yeowell

From VERTIGO
Suggested for
mature readers.

From DC COMICS

BATMAN: ARKHAM ASYLUM
With Dave McKean

JLA: EARTH 2
With Frank Quitely

JLA: NEW WORLD ORDER
With Howard Porter and John Dell

JLA: AMERICAN DREAMS
With Howard Porter, John Dell
and various

JLA: ROCK OF AGES
With Howard Porter, John Dell
and various

JLA: ONE MILLION
With Val Semeiks, Prentis Rollins
and various

ALL VERTIGO TITLES ARE SUGGESTED FOR MATURE READERS

100 BULLETS
Brian Azzarello/Eduardo Risso
With one special briefcase, Agent Graves gives you the chance to kill without retribution. But what is the real price for this chance — and who is setting it?

Vol 1: FIRST SHOT, LAST CALL
Vol 2: SPLIT SECOND CHANCE
Vol 3: HANG UP ON THE HANG LOW
Vol 4: A FOREGONE TOMORROW
Vol 5: THE COUNTERFIFTH DETECTIVE
Vol 6: SIX FEET UNDER THE GUN
Vol 7: SAMURAI

AMERICAN CENTURY
Howard Chaykin/David Tischman/
Marc Laming/John Stokes
The 1950s were no picnic, but for a sharp operator like Harry Kraft opportunity still knocked all over the world — and usually brought trouble right through the door with it.

Vol 1: SCARS & STRIPES
Vol 2: HOLLYWOOD BABYLON

THE BOOKS OF MAGIC
Neil Gaiman/various
A quartet of fallen mystics introduce the world of magic to young Tim Hunter, who is destined to become the world's most powerful magician.

THE BOOKS OF MAGIC
John Ney Rieber/Peter Gross/various
The continuing trials and adventures of Tim Hunter, whose magical talents bring extra trouble and confusion to his adolescence.

Vol 1: BINDINGS
Vol 2: SUMMONINGS
Vol 3: RECKONINGS
Vol 4: TRANSFORMATIONS
Vol 5: GIRL IN THE BOX
Vol 6: THE BURNING GIRL
Vol 7: DEATH AFTER DEATH

DEATH: AT DEATH'S DOOR
Jill Thompson
Part fanciful *manga* retelling of the acclaimed THE SANDMAN: SEASON OF MISTS and part original story of the party from Hell.

DEATH: THE HIGH COST OF LIVING
Neil Gaiman/Chris Bachalo/
Mark Buckingham
One day every century, Death assumes mortal form to learn more about the lives she must take.

DEATH: THE TIME OF YOUR LIFE
Neil Gaiman/Chris Bachalo/
Mark Buckingham/Mark Pennington
A young lesbian mother strikes a deal with Death for the life of her son in a story about fame, relationships, and rock and roll.

FABLES
Bill Willingham/Lan Medina/
Mark Buckingham/Steve Leialoha
The immortal characters of popular fairy tales have been driven from their homelands, and now live hidden among us, trying to cope with life in 21st-century Manhattan.

Vol 1: LEGENDS IN EXILE
Vol 2: ANIMAL FARM
Vol 3: STORYBOOK LOVE

HELLBLAZER
Jamie Delano/Garth Ennis/Warren Ellis/
Brian Azzarello/Steve Dillon/
Marcelo Frusin/various
Where horror, dark magic, and bad luck meet, John Constantine is never far away.

ORIGINAL SINS
DANGEROUS HABITS
FEAR AND LOATHING
TAINTED LOVE
DAMNATION'S FLAME
RAKE AT THE GATES OF HELL
SON OF MAN
HAUNTED
SETTING SUN
HARD TIME
GOOD INTENTIONS
FREEZES OVER
HIGHWATER
RARE CUTS
ALL HIS ENGINES

LUCIFER
Mike Carey/Peter Gross/
Scott Hampton/Chris Weston/
Dean Ormston/various
Walking out of Hell (and out of the pages of THE SANDMAN), an ambitious Lucifer Morningstar creates a new cosmos modeled after his own image.

Vol 1: DEVIL IN THE GATEWAY
Vol 2: CHILDREN AND MONSTERS
Vol 3: A DALLIANCE WITH THE DAMNED
Vol 4: THE DIVINE COMEDY
Vol 5: INFERNO
Vol 6: MANSIONS OF THE SILENCE

PREACHER
Garth Ennis/Steve Dillon/various
A modern American epic of life, death, God, love, and redemption — filled with sex, booze, and blood.

Vol 1: GONE TO TEXAS
Vol 2: UNTIL THE END OF THE WORLD
Vol 3: PROUD AMERICANS
Vol 4: ANCIENT HISTORY
Vol 5: DIXIE FRIED
Vol 6: WAR IN THE SUN
Vol 7: SALVATION
Vol 8: ALL HELL'S A-COMING
Vol 9: ALAMO

THE SANDMAN
Neil Gaiman/various
One of the most acclaimed and celebrated comics titles ever published.

Vol 1: PRELUDES & NOCTURNES
Vol 2: THE DOLL'S HOUSE
Vol 3: DREAM COUNTRY
Vol 4: SEASON OF MISTS
Vol 5: A GAME OF YOU
Vol 6: FABLES & REFLECTIONS
Vol 7: BRIEF LIVES
Vol 8: WORLDS' END
Vol 9: THE KINDLY ONES
Vol 10: THE WAKE
Vol 11: ENDLESS NIGHTS

SWAMP THING: DARK GENESIS
Len Wein/Berni Wrightson
A gothic nightmare is brought to life with this horrifying yet poignant story of a m transformed into a monster.

SWAMP THING
Alan Moore/Stephen Bissette/
John Totleben/Rick Veitch/various
The writer and the series that revolution comics — a masterpiece of lyrical fantasy

Vol 1: SAGA OF THE SWAMP THING
Vol 2: LOVE & DEATH
Vol 3: THE CURSE
Vol 4: A MURDER OF CROWS
Vol 5: EARTH TO EARTH
Vol 6: REUNION
Vol 7: REGENESIS

TRANSMETROPOLITAN
Warren Ellis/Darick Robertson/various
An exuberant trip into a frenetic futu where outlaw journalist Spider Jerusal battles hypocrisy, corruption, and sobrie

Vol 1: BACK ON THE STREET
Vol 2: LUST FOR LIFE
Vol 3: YEAR OF THE BASTARD
Vol 4: THE NEW SCUM
Vol 5: LONELY CITY
Vol 6: GOUGE AWAY
Vol 7: SPIDER'S THRASH
Vol 8: DIRGE
Vol 9: THE CURE
Vol 10: ONE MORE TIME
Vol 0: TALES OF HUMAN WASTE

Y: THE LAST MAN
Brian K. Vaughan/Pia Guerra/
José Marzán, Jr.
An unexplained plague kills every male ma mal on Earth — all except Yorick Brown his pet monkey. Will he survive this n emasculated world to discover what killed fellow men?

Vol 1: UNMANNED
Vol 2: CYCLES
Vol 3: ONE SMALL STEP
Vol 4: SAFEWORD

BARNUM!
Howard Chaykin/David Tischman/
Niko Henrichon

BLACK ORCHID
Neil Gaiman/Dave McKean

GODDESS
Garth Ennis/Phil Winslade

HEAVY LIQUID
Paul Pope

HUMAN TARGET
Peter Milligan/Edvin Biukovic

HUMAN TARGET: FINAL CUT
Peter Milligan/Javier Pulido

HUMAN TARGET: STRIKE ZONES
Peter Milligan/Javier Pulido

I DIE AT MIDNIGHT
Kyle Baker

IN THE SHADOW OF EDGAR ALLAN POE
Jonathon Scott Fuqua/
Stephen John Phillips/Steven Parke

IT'S A BIRD...
Steven T. Seagle/Teddy Kristiansen

JONNY DOUBLE
Brian Azzarello/Eduardo Risso

KING DAVID
Kyle Baker

THE LOSERS: ANTE UP
Andy Diggle/Jock

LOVECRAFT
Hans Rodionoff/Keith Giffen/
Enrique Breccia

MR. PUNCH
Neil Gaiman/Dave McKean

THE MYSTERY PLAY
Grant Morrison/Jon J Muth

THE NAMES OF MAGIC
Dylan Horrocks/Richard Case

**NEIL GAIMAN & CHARLES VESS'
STARDUST**
Neil Gaiman/Charles Vess

NEIL GAIMAN'S MIDNIGHT DAYS
Neil Gaiman/Matt Wagner/various

ORBITER
Warren Ellis/Colleen Doran

**PREACHER: DEAD OR ALIVE
(THE COLLECTED COVERS)**
Glenn Fabry

PRIDE & JOY
Garth Ennis/John Higgins

PROPOSITION PLAYER
Bill Willingham/Paul Guinan/Ron Randall

**THE SANDMAN:
THE DREAM HUNTERS**
Neil Gaiman/Yoshitaka Amano

**THE SANDMAN: DUST COVERS — THE
COLLECTED SANDMAN COVERS 1989–1997**
Dave McKean/Neil Gaiman

THE SANDMAN PRESENTS: THE FURIES
Mike Carey/John Bolton

**THE SANDMAN PRESENTS:
TALLER TALES**
Bill Willingham/various

**SHADE, THE CHANGING MAN:
THE AMERICAN SCREAM**
Peter Milligan/Chris Bachalo

UNCLE SAM
Steve Darnall/Alex Ross

UNDERCOVER GENIE
Kyle Baker

UNKNOWN SOLDIER
Garth Ennis/Kilian Plunkett

V FOR VENDETTA
Alan Moore/David Lloyd

VEILS
Pat McGreal/Stephen John Phillips/
José Villarrubia

WHY I HATE SATURN
Kyle Baker

THE WITCHING HOUR
Jeph Loeb/Chris Bachalo/Art Thiber

YOU ARE HERE
Kyle Baker
